BUSINESS
SELLING
INSIGHTS
VOL. 8

BUSINESS
SELLING
INSIGHTS

VOL. 8

SPOTLIGHTS ON LEADING BUSINESS INTERMEDIARIES, BROKERS, AND M&A ADVISORS

FEATURING LEADING BUSINESS INTERMEDIARIES, BROKERS, AND M&A ADVISORS

Kingsley Allison

Brent Engelbrekt

Chris George

Darrow Graham

Katherine Harris

Jim Nairn

Jim M. Peake

Yatin Thakore

Claudio Vilas

Business Selling Insights Vol. 8/ Mark Imperial

Managing Editor/ Shannon Buritz

ISBN:978-1-954757-49-3

CONTENTS

A NOTE TO THE READER

Thank you for obtaining your copy of "BUSINESS SELLING INSIGHTS Vol. 8: Spotlights on Leading Business Intermediaries, Brokers, and M&A Advisors." This book was originally created as a series of live interviews; that's why it reads like a series of conversations, rather than a traditional book that talks at you.

My team and I have personally invited these professionals to share their knowledge because they have demonstrated that they are true advocates for the success of their clients and have shown their great ability to educate the public on the topic of buying and selling businesses.

I wanted you to feel as though the participants and I are talking with you, much like a close friend or relative, and felt that creating the material this way would make it easier for you to grasp the topics and put them to use quickly, rather than wading through hundreds of pages.

So relax, grab a pen and paper, take notes, and get ready to learn some fascinating insights from our Leading Business Intermediaries, Brokers, and M&A Advisors.

Warmest regards,

Mark Imperial
Publisher, Author, and Radio Personality

INTRODUCTION

"BUSINESS SELLING INSIGHTS Vol. 8: Spotlights on Leading Business Intermediaries, Brokers, and M&A Advisors" is a collaborative book series featuring leading professionals from across the country.

Remarkable Press™ would like to extend a heartfelt thank you to all participants who took the time to submit their chapter and offer their support in becoming ambassadors for this project.

100% of the royalties from this book's retail sales will be donated to the Global Autism Project. Should you want to make a direct donation, visit their website at GlobalAutismProject.org

KINGSLEY ALLISON

SERVICE SUCCESS: EXPERT TIPS FOR SELLING YOUR SERVICE BUSINESS

Conversation with Kingsley Allison

Kingsley Allison is an excellent resource for service business owners considering selling. Specializing in businesses valued from $500,000 to $5 million, Kingsley helps owners prepare and plan for a successful sale. This interview explores the challenges of selling a service business and how Kingsley guides owners. He shares his methods for making the sale process smoother, explains some common myths about business sales, and offers practical advice that any service business owner can use.

■ **Tell us about your work and the people you help.**

Kingsley Allison: I'm a business broker. I specialize in selling service businesses between $500,000 and $5 million. Many of the business owners I work with reach a point where they need to finance or move on. They may be looking for a strategic buyer if their business has grown but is not big enough for an investor to buy. So, I help them take a family business and move it up to the next level.

■ **What is the biggest challenge these service business owners face? How do you help them overcome this challenge?**

Kingsley Allison: The biggest challenge is not having an exit plan. They usually come to me when things stop working, and I work with them to get things back on track so they can have a smooth transition and realize the full effect of the business. By the time they come to me, they are already burned out. They feel they have had enough and are ready to get rid of the business. And I say, "Okay, I understand that the business has been going down the last three years because you are tired. But now, what can we do to smooth things out?" Once you smooth things out, it will be an easier transition.

■ **When is the best time to sell a business?**

Kingsley Allison: The best time to sell a business is when you have a buyer, and it's on an upswing. You can make your best deal on an upswing.

■ **Are there common myths and misconceptions about selling a business?**

Kingsley Allison: One is that the value of your business is a multiple of the cash flow. There's so much more to a business than just cash flow. There are intellectual property and market conditions. Is the industry leveling off? Not to mention, there is the value of goodwill. Goodwill is sometimes even better than cash flow.

Business owners also often fail to consider what the next buyer wants. They believe that whatever they are doing, the buyer will follow in their footsteps. But that's not always the case.

■ **What common mistakes or pitfalls do you help sellers avoid?**

Kingsley Allison: Sellers tend to talk too much. Sometimes, they say, "I won't take a penny less than _____ for my business." This reveals their hand. Or they might say, "I've been running this business for 30 years, but now I want to get out because of X, Y, and Z, or my rent skyrocketed," which scares potential buyers off.

Sometimes, sellers think that once they put the business on the market, they can head off to Tahiti and stop working on it. But when a business is on the market, it is crucial to put in the work and ensure that it continues running smoothly.

Sellers also often need to plan more for what comes next after the sale. What will their next chapter of life look like?

■ What inspired you to get started in this field?

Kingsley Allison: I worked for a manufacturer testing equipment in a factory. I would often travel to different customer sites, and I always ran into the same guy. One morning, I said to him, "I keep seeing you. What do you do?" He said, "I'm a business broker, and I help business owners sell their businesses." I credit him for putting the bug about business brokerage in my ear. I started learning all I could about the industry, got hired as a broker, and have enjoyed this work ever since.

■ Is there anything else you want to share with business owners considering selling?

Kingsley Allison: Business owners often try to "time the market," thinking it might be better next year or in five years. You can't predict the market. The best time to sell is *now*.

■ **How can people find you, connect with you, and learn more?**

Kingsley Allison: Every business is different, so it's important to have a conversation about your unique business. My website is www. linkbusiness.com, or you can call me directly at 914-363-7731.

KINGSLEY ALLISON

Business Broker

LINK Business, New York City

Kingsley Allison is a seasoned expert in the valuation and sale of privately held businesses, specializing in guiding business owners through the most critical transactions of their careers, with a Master's degree in Business Administration and over 25 years of dedicated service. He brings his wealth of experience and expertise to LINK Business, New York City, where he is excited to continue making a significant impact. Whether you are buying or selling a business, Kingsley is eager to address your questions and assist you every step of the way.

EMAIL:
kingsley.allison@linkbusiness.com

PHONE:
914-363-7731

WEBSITE:
linkbusiness.com

LINKEDIN:
https://www.linkedin.com/in/kingsley-allison-12937313/

BRENT
ENGELBREKT

TRUE NORTH TO A SUCCESSFUL EXIT

Conversation with Brent Engelbrekt

Exiting a business can be one of the most significant and challenging decisions a business owner will ever make. Brent Engelbrekt, the Managing Director of True North Mergers & Acquisitions, is dedicated to guiding business owners through this complex journey. With a wealth of experience in industrials, including manufacturing, distribution, and engineering companies, Brent and his team provide the expertise and support necessary to ensure a successful transition. In this interview, Brent shares his insights on the common challenges, misconceptions, and pitfalls that business owners face when considering an exit and his personal journey into the field of mergers and acquisitions.

■ **Brent, you are the Managing Director of True North Mergers & Acquisitions. Tell us about your work and the people you help.**

Brent Engelbrekt: We help business owners who are starting to think about selling their business. They often don't know what is involved. We walk them through the process, help determine the right time to sell, and take them to market. Ideally, we come out on the other end with a successful sale that everyone is happy about.

■ **Are there any specific types of businesses you specialize in?**

Brent Engelbrekt: We focus on industrials, a broad category that encompasses manufacturing, distribution, and engineering companies.

■ **What is the biggest challenge your clients face? How do you help overcome this challenge?**

Brent Engelbrekt: The most common questions are "Is it the right time?" and "What is the rest of my life going to look like?" Sometimes, they have thought this through, and sometimes, they haven't. It's our job to help them psychologically understand what they are trying to accomplish.

Many business owners fear the exit process because they don't understand it. A large part of our role is providing education to alleviate this fear.

■ Are there common myths and misconceptions about exiting a business?

Brent Engelbrekt: There are many misconceptions about how to value a business. Someone might hear from their buddy at the country club that they received 10x or 20x multiple for their business and assume they can do the same. However, each business is unique and requires an individualized valuation.

Business owners also need clarification about the economy and how it impacts the sale. Sometimes, the macro environment can hurt the seller, but if they have a strong business that performs well and is not subject to the ups and downs of the economy, it still might be a great time to sell.

■ What mistakes or pitfalls do you help people avoid when exiting their business?

Brent Engelbrekt: One of the biggest mistakes is being unprepared for unexpected life events. Scenarios like death and divorce can quickly derail a successful business if the owner doesn't work to maximize the business's value ahead of time.

■ Brent, what inspired you to get started in this field?

Brent Engelbrekt: I've always had a strong financial background and owned different companies. Most recently, about ten years ago, I sold a manufacturing services company to a private equity group, ran it for a year, got paid for another year, and wasn't ready to retire. This is something I've always liked. I enjoy it, and it's an excellent lifestyle business.

■ Is there anything else you want to share with business owners considering an exit?

Brent Engelbrekt: In many ways, I consider myself a coach. Conversations with business owners about exiting can take a few years to come to fruition. I take pride in helping people make corrections to achieve greater success a few years down the road. It's a true advisory type of role. And I have the real-life experience to back it up. There is a psychological aspect to helping business owners through the exit process.

■ **How can people find you, connect with you, and learn more?**

Brent Engelbrekt: Feel free to contact me on our website: www. tnma.com.

BRENT ENGELBREKT, CBI, M&AMI, CM&AP, CEPA

Managing Director

True North Mergers & Acquisitions

As a past business owner, Brent comes with a key understanding of the business sales process. He acquired this knowledge firsthand as a principal in several successful business and commercial real estate transactions. Brent knows what it takes to present a business for sale properly. He understands the motivations of buyers and sellers and exactly how to cut through the clutter and focus on what matters: a successful transaction that feels right for both parties. Whether you are ready to sell now or in the future, no one will work harder and with more integrity to guide you through the process.

Brent is a Certified Business Intermediary (CBI) and a Mergers and Acquisitions Master Intermediary (M&AMI), both formal designations bestowed on him by the International Business Brokers Association (IBBA) and its sister organization, the M&A Source. In addition, he holds a Certified M&A Professional (CM&AP) designation from Coles College M&A Academy at Kennesaw State University in Georgia. He is a Certified Exit Planning Advisor (CEPA), a designation earned through the Exit Planning Institute (EPI), a worldwide organization dedicated to delivering consistently better outcomes to business owners seeking to unlock the wealth they have built up in their businesses.

Brent was named the 2021 CBI of the Year in May 2022 at the annual IBBA Conference in Denver. In addition, he earned the IBBA 2021 Platinum Chairman's Circle Award and was named to the M&A Source Platinum Club for the third year in a row.

Prior to joining True North Mergers and Acquisitions, Brent was an owner and Senior Vice President at RIE Coatings, where he and his team grew the business from $3 million to $10 million in sales from 2009 to 2013 and were instrumental in selling the company to a Twin Cities-based private equity group in 2024. Brent has a bachelor's degree in business administration from Minnesota State

University in Mankato with a concentration in Marketing and Finance and a minor in Economics.

EMAIL:

bengelbrekt@tnma.com

PHONE:

(612) 455-0886

CHRIS
GEORGE

THE FRANCHISE MAVERICK

Conversation with Chris George

Chris George, founder and senior broker with Franchise Maverick, has dedicated his career to guiding people through the complexities of franchising. With over two decades of experience as a franchisee, Chris brings a wealth of knowledge and a unique perspective to his role. In this interview, Chris discusses the dual facets of his work: the buy side, where he aids individuals in identifying and acquiring the right franchise, and the resale side, where he supports franchisees in selling their businesses effectively. He also talks about the common challenges franchise buyers and sellers face, sharing advice on overcoming these hurdles. Whether you're considering entering the franchise world or looking to sell your franchise, Chris' insights offer a comprehensive guide to making better, more informed strategic decisions.

■ **Chris, you are the founder and senior franchise broker with Franchise Maverick. Tell us about your work and the people you help.**

Chris George: I have two primary focuses in my work within the franchising space. The first is working with individuals, aspiring entrepreneurs, and existing entrepreneurs who want to explore franchise opportunities. These opportunities could be new startups or acquiring an existing franchise business. So that's the buy side of the equation.

On the resale side, my focus is helping current franchisees sell their businesses. Right now, I am focused on restaurants and home services, though I have the expertise to help those in any franchise sector. The restaurant space is my background. I was a franchisee with a major QSR franchise brand for over two decades. That led me down this path after I sold my own businesses. I saw a way to leverage my experience and expertise to add value and serve both franchise candidates and franchisees trying to sell their current business.

In the case of selling an existing franchise business, it's key to understand that in addition to the variables you contend with in selling any business, there is also a third party in the deal, the franchisor. When pre-qualifying buyers, you have to qualify them in two ways: first, financially and motivationally as it relates to buying any business. And then whether they are a good fit for the franchise brand.

In a franchise resale, in the vast majority of cases, the buyer, whether already a franchisee or becoming a new franchisee, will have to sign a new agreement and be awarded the franchise. So, they will have to go through the process that the franchisor has in place. Additionally, the entire sale or transfer will be subject to franchisor approval.

■ What are the biggest challenges new franchisees face? How do you help them overcome these challenges?

Chris George: A candidate on the buy side faces several challenges. There are roughly 4,000 franchises at any given time, making it a massive undertaking to identify the right options that are available, connect with the brand, and complete due diligence. It's also a highly regulated industry. Candidates can easily disqualify themselves from consideration by simply not understanding how to properly navigate the process.

Reflecting on my own career as a franchisee, I made my share of mistakes. I started very young, at 22, and didn't know there were people out there who could help me navigate this world more efficiently. One of the biggest mistakes of new investors or buyers is buying into what they know. Maybe they're a customer of a business and like it, but owning that business is not the same as being a customer. Or, they falsely believe they have to have experience in the industry and only evaluate those options. I've seen people invest in franchises that were not a good fit because they didn't have the proper perspective. As a result, some fail, and others find themselves dissatisfied and no happier or better off than before they started their business.

At the core of franchising, it's all about systems and support. You need the right leadership and systems in place. That's what you're buying into. So, why not use a strategic system to evaluate and identify the right franchise for you? What's right for me may not be right for you. The question becomes, do you have or are you following a proven system to identify the best fit for you? This goes to the heart of answering why you want to invest in a franchise. Why start a business in the first place, and why franchising? If you're entering this space with a particular industry or brand in mind, why that brand or industry? Have you explored other industries or brands? Why or why not?

Generally, people don't understand franchising. Their initial reasons for choosing a particular industry or brand are based on a lack of information and misconceptions. The biggest challenge when I work with candidates on the front end is getting past those initial misperceptions. My first step is to help you determine whether franchising makes sense for you and then clarify your ideal business based on various factors.

We'll inventory your skill sets and create a profile of the perfect business. While a perfect business doesn't exist, we can create a template. I then apply this template across multiple databases to identify the business models that make the most sense based on your criteria. I then confirm territory availability so that we have an understanding of what that looks like. We will review the best matches together before you connect with the franchisors, saving you a lot of time.

I'll make introductions to the brands you want to know more about. I work directly with franchise reps, so you get priority treatment from the start. It's analogous to applying for jobs. If a hiring manager gets a referred candidate from a trusted source, they'll look at that resume first. Similarly, in franchising, a direct introduction from me means the franchisor knows I've spent time with you and believe you are a good candidate for them. This upfront matchmaking is a significant advantage over going directly to the franchisor, where your application might get lost among hundreds or thousands of others. Additionally, I provide ongoing support and advocacy to help you through due diligence, funding, and award process.

■ What are the biggest challenges sellers face? How do you help them overcome these challenges?

Chris George: Business brokers have found that sellers tend to over-value their businesses based on their gut feeling and the blood, sweat, and tears invested. And I get it; I've been there myself. However, in franchising, I've seen many franchisees undervalue their businesses, especially when selling to other franchisees in the system.

When I sold my first two locations, I sold them to other franchisees without any intermediaries other than an attorney. We never got valuations; it was just based on what we thought the business might be worth, often influenced by deals we had seen other franchisees make. The problem with this approach is that we were operating in a bubble, similar to selling a house without putting it on the open market, potentially not maximizing its value. And, in my case, I handled most of the transactional components because I was comfortable with contracts and documents. This made things easier, but it didn't mean I realized full value or protection in the transaction.

When selling my third restaurant, the buyer pool in my locality had dried up, especially during COVID. I had to look outside the system, which led me to hiring a business broker specializing in franchising. With the broker's help, I was able to command a much higher valuation than I had received internally. Even after paying the success fee to the broker, I still cleared more than the highest internal offer. This experience validated what the broker shared with me. Many franchisees may be undervaluing their business by keeping the sale within the ranks.

Another misconception is that it will be easy to sell. It's a major transaction with a lot of moving parts and details that have to be resolved in a timely manner and at the right time intervals. I don't think I can overstate the significance of the transaction. Most of us don't think twice about hiring a real estate professional to help us buy or sell a home. We recognize the magnitude of the transaction and its implications. Buying or selling a business is no less a major transaction with substantial implications.

Here's how I help sellers overcome these challenges. First, I provide them with a valuation that accurately reflects the most probable selling price in an open market for their business.

Second, I have an exclusive network of brokers who represent franchise buyers. This group of buyers may not be looking for businesses on traditional resale platforms. And, because I'm willing to co-broker these deals, sellers gain an extended sales force.

Third, my experience working with franchise buyers is an advantage for the seller. I understand the franchise buyer mindset and the types of candidates the franchisors are seeking. This is important because we are looking for a particular type of buyer. We are looking for buyers who can satisfy the franchisor's approval process and are qualified and motivated.

■ What mistakes or pitfalls should people avoid when trying to overcome these challenges?

Chris George: One of the biggest mistakes people make is waiting to sell until it's too late. I always think of the quote from the movie American Gangster when the Chinese general tells Frank that "quitting while you're ahead is not the same as quitting." Sometimes, people go through these up-and-down cycles when considering selling but don't explore the options.

I decided to sell my last restaurant when I recognized that I didn't have the drive to take it to the next level. I was comfortable, but not in a good way. That was the turning point for me. I had achieved a lot at that point in terms of growth and profitability, so it made sense to sell at this peak. The risk of waiting might mean my lack of full engagement could slowly erode the key value drivers and ultimately devalue the business.

It's better to give yourself at least a year or two of preparation to sell. It allows time to work with your broker to find ways to increase the value of your business and prepare it to go to market.

■ **What challenges do you often encounter with your services?**

Chris George: The biggest challenge I encounter with sellers, and one that I wrestled with myself, is skepticism about the need for a broker. This stems from a concern over the success fee and a fear that once the sale is finalized, you might look back and think, "I could have done that myself and saved money." That was what I thought when I sold my first two locations. When I sold the last location with a broker, I was apprehensive about the process for many of those reasons. However, I was very pleased with the buyer he found and surprised at how much easier the entire process went.

It's similar on the buy side. Many buyers are skeptical that they need help finding a good franchise and suspect I'm just trying to sell them something or will limit their options. I chose a brand without expert guidance or a systematic process and learned firsthand the consequences of choosing without a quality process and good information. My role isn't to sell you anything - that's the franchise rep's job. My role is to equip you to make a better, more informed decision and support you through the process of due diligence so that you can make the choice you believe is best for you.

■ What inspired you to get into this line of work?

Chris George: I have a passion for business and entrepreneurship. I'm a strong believer in franchising as a path to business ownership, and I have always wanted to help people achieve better outcomes in their small businesses. I made a lot of mistakes in my journey, some of which were very costly financially and emotionally. I want to help others avoid those same mistakes.

I also learned the value of expertise and wise counsel. My default is to DIY, and that applies to just about everything! I've considered re-roofing my house, insulating my basement, upholstering my car seats, and so many other projects! But I discovered years ago that when I started to engage others' expertise, I was able to achieve more, faster, and with better outcomes.

Finally, I'm actually quite competitive and enjoy the deal-making process. My core strengths in accounting, financial analysis, negotiation, and creative problem solving, combined with my competitive nature and enjoyment of deal-making, make this line of work a perfect fit. Helping others buy and sell businesses is rewarding for me.

■ **Is there anything else you would like to share?**

Chris George: I work with over 800 franchises across more than 30 sectors. So, when it comes to exploring startup opportunities, evaluating good bolt-on businesses, diversifying your current business holdings, or selling your franchised business, I can help!

■ **How can people find you, connect with you, and learn more?**

Chris George: You can reach me by phone or text at 205-797-0733, by email at cgeorge@franchisemaverick.com, and on LinkedIn at https://www.linkedin.com/in/cageorge/

CHRIS GEORGE

Broker-Owner, FSC, MBA

Franchise Maverick

Chris discovered his passion for entrepreneurship in his teens. After several short-lived ventures, he found a perfect fit in franchising, leading to a successful career spanning over two decades as a multi-unit franchisee and brand leader with a national QSR restaurant brand. This journey allowed him to achieve his personal, business, and financial goals while positively impacting his community, employees, and customers. This embodies his "American Dream."

Today, Chris is dedicated to helping others achieve their "American Dream" through all stages of franchise business ownership. He believes that franchising offers a unique opportunity to achieve success in business. For individuals seeking to launch their first business or diversify their current portfolio, Chris serves as a trusted advisor and advocate, helping them identify and launch the right franchise business for them.

For those seeking to sell their established franchise businesses, Chris provides resale services tailored to the franchise process and access to an exclusive franchise buyer network.

In either case, his experience, expertise, and resource partnerships ensure his clients are empowered to make informed decisions, achieve better results, and realize their goals and dreams.

Chris opened his first franchised restaurant at age 22 and later expanded to multiple units, earned numerous brand awards, and served in various leadership roles. He holds an M.B.A., is a licensed REALTOR®, and is Franchise Sales Compliant. In his spare time, Chris enjoys traveling, reading, writing, and all things franchising.

EMAIL:
cgeorge@franchisemaverick.com

PHONE:
205-797-0733

WEBSITE:
www.franchisemaverick.com

LINKEDIN:
https://www.linkedin.com/in/cageorge/

DARROW
GRAHAM

PREPARING FOR THE SELLER TSUNAMI

Conversation with Darrow Graham

Darrow Graham is a business advisor with Transworld Business Advisors, headquartered in Florida. Since acquiring his franchise in 2017, he has contributed to making Transworld the largest brokerage firm in the United States. Specializing in upper Main Street deals, Darrow focuses on businesses with top-line revenues ranging from $1 million to $10 million. His extensive experience has positioned him as a valuable resource for business owners looking to transition for various reasons, including retirement, health issues, or other personal circumstances. In this interview, Darrow shares his insights on valuing and selling businesses, common misconceptions, and his approach to guiding clients through the process of selling their business.

■ **Darrow, you are a business advisor with Transworld Business Advisors. Tell us about your work and the people you help.**

Darrow Graham: Transworld is franchised, and I bought the Grapevine territory here in Dallas-Fort Worth in 2017. We're now the largest brokerage firm in the United States. We focus on Main Street and upper Main Street deals. That means generally any business with a top-line revenue from $50,000 up to $10 million. We're helping business owners looking to transition for various reasons. It can be retirement, burnout, health-related issues, divorce, or needing to move. Many of the people we're helping right now are baby boomers at an age where they're ready to retire and transition their legacy to another owner.

■ **What is the biggest challenge your clients face? How do you help them overcome this challenge?**

Darrow Graham: The biggest challenge for owners is helping them understand how we determine the value of their business. The value is not up to me or the owner; it's what the market will bear. It's whatever the owner is willing to sell it for, and the buyer is willing to buy it for. A lot of times, because someone has worked in the business their entire lives or their CPA or financial advisor gave them a number, they have an unrealistic expectation of its value. It has a lot to do with what other businesses in the industry and of similar size sell for, which is very similar to how homes are sold. This is called the market approach. We focus a lot of our time on helping owners understand where the market is and the range of value where transactions are happening.

■ Are there common myths and misconceptions about selling a business?

Darrow Graham: Sellers are experts in running and growing their businesses. But, they are not experts in selling their business. When we encounter business owners trying to sell their business while running it, the business suffers because they are overwhelmed by everything required to take it to the marketplace and manage all the buyer inquiries, many of which are unqualified to purchase it. Unsolicited buyers show up unannounced during business hours, and their employees find out. In some cases, employees leave because they fear the new owner will bring in their own team to run the business, and they will have to find another job. A business needs to show stability and growth. Trying to sell it while running it does not work.

Only 20% of businesses sell annually. It is closer to 10% if you follow the data. The other 80%, or 90%, are generally overpriced, or their financials are hard to follow. Many business owners equate longevity with value or have talked to a CPA who is excellent at taxes but not qualified to value a business. Buyers are much more sophisticated these days and generally will not pay more than 15% over the market price for a business unless it is strategic, fits geographically, or diversifies their product mix.

■ How long does it typically take to sell a business?

Darrow Graham: The national average for selling a business is nine to twelve months. I always tell people, "You never know when the real buyer will show up." About 95% of all buyers who inquire about a business don't end up buying it. We have processes in place to weed out unqualified buyers, and we engage prospective buyers with confidentiality agreements and financial qualifications. If it qualifies with an SBA lender, it will add another 45 to 60 days to the timeline to sell. We develop a detailed confidential information memorandum or CIM that tells a great story about the owner, the business, its history, financial information, and opportunities for growth. If it's priced right, we have a much higher likelihood of getting really good inquiries when we roll it out, and it will sell quickly.

■ When is the best time to sell a business?

Darrow Graham: That's a tricky question; the answer depends on the seller. What is their true "why"—why do they want to sell? If we have a motivated seller, we will find a motivated buyer. The best time to sell is when sales are up and profitable. However, as I mentioned, there are other motivating factors when a business owner decides to sell. There are economic factors to consider as well. COVID was a global economic crisis, and many companies have still not recovered. Some areas of the country fare better than others. Texas is one of the hottest markets in the country, literally! Bi-coastal migration into the state, low regulations, favorable business environment, and availability of capital indicate that it is a great time to sell your business in Texas.

The number of businesses for sale can also affect the timing of when to sell. One thing we see on the horizon is the "seller tsunami." This will be the largest transfer of wealth in our nation's history, with many baby boomers exiting their businesses at the same time. This will increase inventory and create more competition for sellers, meaning they may have to lower their purchase price to sell. If someone is considering selling within the next year or so, they need to talk to a broker and start working through the process. It's still a seller's market, but when inventory increases dramatically, business owners will likely have to decrease their price points to sell a business.

■ What mistakes or pitfalls should people be aware of when selling their business?

Darrow Graham: One of the biggest mistakes is when owners tell their employees they are selling their business. This happens often when they try to sell it on their own. Confidentiality is a big deal in selling a business because you don't want your employees, vendors, or customers to know. Owners stop investing in the typical day-to-day operations like marketing, equipment, and vehicle maintenance or depleting inventory below normal levels to conserve cash. It may take up to a year to sell, and buyers will walk away if sales and service go down because the owner is purposely divesting in running the business.

■ What are the most commonly asked questions from sellers?

Darrow Graham: "What is my business worth? Do you think it's sellable? Who is the buyer going to be? Is it going to be another company? Would it be a strategic buy from another organization?"

The majority of the buyers are first-time business owners. Many have just left the corporate world, have managed a business, and want to start their own. They always have questions about how the buyer will finance the business and the pitfalls around seller financing. It actually makes the business more sellable, and the failure rate is very low, if done right.

■ Please give us a brief overview of what it is like to work with you.

Darrow Graham: First, we want to meet with the seller in person, either at our office for confidentiality or in a private place at their business. We want to sit down with them and understand their business—how they got started, the history, the challenges, and the opportunities. It's crucial to determine why they want to sell. If they're motivated to sell, the next step is to perform a business valuation, for which we don't charge any upfront fees. We'll create a 30-page report comparing them against other businesses in their industry of similar size and profit along with their business performance.

If they need help getting their financials in order, we can refer them to CPAs and bookkeepers, as we need that information for a proper business valuation. We then sit down with the owner, go through the valuation, and explain how we come up with a range of values, not an exact number. If the seller is motivated by those numbers, we proceed to the marketplace. We develop all the marketing materials and list the business on all the top listing sites worldwide, including over 250 Transworld offices.

We ensure the listing is confidential. People will know the county it's in but not the business's name or location. We then develop the confidential information memorandum (CIM), a detailed report with all financial information, history, operations, employees, and market strategy that tells a great story about the business.

When buyers start to inquire, they sign a nondisclosure agreement before we send out the CIM. I get on a call with prospective buyers to ensure they have the financial capacity, good credit, and relevant experience. If they pass, we send them the CIM and go through it. If all goes well, we set up a buyer-seller meeting, usually after hours at the location, allowing for a facility tour and an interview between buyer and seller. They must trust each other for the deal to work.

If the meeting goes well, we ask the buyer to make an offer. If accepted, we go under contract, and generally, we close the transaction within 30 to 60 days.

■ Darrow, what inspired you to get started in this field?

Darrow Graham: I owned a business for ten years in the apartment industry. We were a wholesale distributor, and I met a lot of business brokers and M&A professionals. I was always fascinated by what they did and got to know many of them. When I transitioned out of my business, I met someone who had purchased a Transworld franchise here in Dallas-Fort Worth. I interviewed them, and they told me a lot about their successes in the business. So I contacted Transworld corporate and bought the Grapevine territory in Dallas-Fort Worth in 2017.

■ Is there anything else you want to share with business owners considering selling?

Darrow Graham: Even if you're not ready to sell now, engaging with a business broker is really important. Many things need to be done to get your house in order before the sale; some of these things take much longer than you would expect. If we can have a conversation, we can advise you on things you can work on. We have a lot of free business development tools at our disposal to help increase the value of your business so you can maximize value in the end.

There are also tax implications. Capital gains and ordinary income can be as high as 35% of the transaction, and we can help. We can assist you in building a team and introduce you to some of our strategic alliances that can help with tax issues or connect you with CPAs to clean up your books. There's a lot that goes into maximizing liquidity at the end.

■ How can people find you, connect with you, and learn more?

Darrow Graham: You can call me on my cell phone at 214-729-2033 or you can shoot me an email at dgraham@tworld.com. You can also find me at tworld.com/grapevine.

J. DARROW GRAHAM

President

Transworld Business Advisors

Transworld Business Advisors is the world leader in the marketing and sales of businesses, franchises, and commercial real estate.
Whether you represent an acquisition-minded corporation or are
personally interested in owning your own company, Transworld

offers the professional services that successfully bring buyers and sellers together. From business brokerage to mergers and acquisitions, we are the business sales specialists.

Since our inception, we have excelled in getting deals done! Contact us and you will understand what makes us the best company to handle any business or commercial real estate sale.

PHONE:
855-528-9735

EMAIL:
dgraham@tworld.com

WEBSITES:
tworld.com/grapevine and Hopeadvisor.com

KATHERINE HARRIS

BRIDGING BUYERS AND SELLERS IN MAIN STREET AND LOWER MIDDLE MARKET TRANSACTIONS

Conversation with Katherine Harris

Katherine Harris is a seasoned business broker and advisor with Apogee Equity Partners, Inc. Operating from their headquarters in South Carolina, she and her team focus on assisting Lower Middle Market and Main Street businesses with revenues ranging from a few hundred thousand to $25 million. Through this interview, Katherine shares her insights on realistic business valuations, the emotional aspects of business transactions, and the strategic preparations necessary for selling a business. Katherine's expertise helps business owners overcome the challenges and embrace the rewards of selling their life's work.

■ **Katherine, you are a business broker with Apogee Equity Partners. Tell us about your work and the people you help.**

Katherine Harris: I am with Apogee Equity Partners. We help buyers and sellers in the lower middle market, typically ranging from $4 million to $25 million in revenue. We also have a division that works with smaller businesses. These businesses can be anywhere from a few hundred thousand to $4 million in revenue. We are geographically and industry agnostic.

■ **What is the biggest challenge your clients face? And how do you help them overcome this challenge?**

Katherine Harris: It's a two-phase challenge. Sellers of Main Street businesses often have misguided value expectations. They might have heard from other business owners that valuations are based on a multiple of revenue, or they may have received advice from someone in a completely different industry. It is important to note that valuation methods vary significantly between large and small businesses and differ by industry type and company size. We strongly recommend that all our clients seek a professional Broker Opinion of Value (BOV) tailored to their specific business.

Many of our clients have dedicated years to growing and nurturing their businesses in the lower middle market. Yet, they often lack clarity regarding their true value and the intricacies of the selling process. We invest substantial time with each client to thoroughly discuss the entire process and elucidate the nuances associated with various types of buyers. Specifically, in this market segment, our buyers are typically private equity firms, high-net-worth individuals, and strategic in nature.

■ What are the biggest myths or misconceptions about selling a business?

Katherine Harris: Many business owners are concerned that a new buyer will alter the company's culture or replace staff. However, most buyers prefer to maintain the existing operations and workforce. While they may have plans for growth, they recognize the value of retaining all employees, particularly in the current labor market. Sellers often develop strong relationships with their employees over many years and deeply care about their well-being, wanting them to thrive post-sale. Frequently, the buyer is a larger company, which can provide employees with even greater opportunities for career advancement.

■ **What is the most significant mistake people make when selling their business? How do you help your clients avoid this mistake?**

Katherine Harris: Business owners often fail to prepare adequately for their business's sale. Ideally, an owner should be able to sell on their terms and within their preferred time frame, such as during retirement or to capitalize on a favorable economic cycle. However, unforeseen circumstances like divorce, illness, or relocation can necessitate a sale. In such cases, advance preparation is invaluable. Beginning the exit process one, two, or even three years in advance is advisable. Consulting with a professional well ahead of time is beneficial, regardless of the owner's current situation. A broker can provide guidance on valuation, preparing financials, management structure, and other factors to ensure your business is attractive to potential buyers. Adequate preparation is crucial to receive maximum value and a smooth transition. The most common mistake business owners make is insufficient preparation before the sale.

■ **Katherine, what inspired you to get into this line of work? How did you get started?**

Katherine Harris: I came from a world of corporate financial analysis and information technology. After doing that for 20 years, my entrepreneurial spirit came alive. I was looking into buying a business.

I walked into Apogee Equity Partners, and instead of buying a business, I walked out with a new career that I enjoy immensely.

■ Is there anything else you would like to share?

Katherine Harris: Apogee Equity Partners operates on a national scale, with offices located in Columbia, South Carolina; Denver, Colorado; and Louisville, Kentucky. Our team is strategically positioned across the United States, including key locations such as Montgomery, Alabama, and San Diego, California. Our Main Street brokerage primarily serves the South Carolina market. A significant portion of Apogee specializes in residential and commercial trade services, including HVAC, plumbing, electrical work, and restoration. We are also very involved in manufacturing, distribution, retail, and commercial construction.

■ How can people find you, connect with you, and learn more?

Katherine Harris: Our websites are ApogeeEquityPartners.com and www.sunbeltnetwork.com/columbia-sc. To contact me directly, email me at katherine@ApogeeEquityPartners.com or call 844-368-6979.

KATHERINE HARRIS, CMSBB, SC AND GA REAL ESTATE LICENSES

~~~~~~~~~~

Business Broker

Apogee Equity Partners, Inc.

Katherine Harris is a highly accomplished and results-driven business broker renowned for her extensive track record in successfully closing numerous transactions. Her unwavering commitment to securing optimal prices and exceptional experiences for her clients distinguishes her as a top-tier professional in the industry.

Before joining Apogee Equity Partners, Katherine honed her business acumen as the Director of Business Integration at a leading manufacturing company. In this pivotal role, she managed the Information Technology, Financial Analysis, and Commercial Operations Groups, demonstrating her expertise in financial management, process optimization, and project leadership.

Katherine's educational background includes a Bachelor's Degree in Finance from the esteemed business school at the University of South Carolina. She also holds the Certified Main Street Business Broker (CMSBB) designation, is active in the International Business Brokers Association (IBBA), and possesses real estate licenses in South Carolina and Georgia. This extensive qualification ensures her clients receive the highest level of expertise and service.

With her wealth of experience and dedication, Katherine is a trusted partner for both buyers and sellers, expertly guiding them through seamless and prosperous transactions.

EMAIL:
katherine@ApogeeEquityPartners.com

PHONE:
844-368-6979

WEBSITES:
ApogeeEquityPartners.com
www.sunbeltnetwork.com/columbia-sc

JIM
NAIRN

THE MASTER OF MANY HATS

Conversation with Jim Nairn

Selling a business requires not one or two but thirty distinct roles to navigate the process successfully. In this interview, we talk with Jim Nairn, a business broker based in Kingston, Ontario, who has mastered these roles. Jim helps business owners understand how the market values their operations, whether now's the right time to sell or if they should buckle down and build upon their enterprise for a few more years to achieve their financial or retirement goals. Specializing in assisting Canadian entrepreneurs whose businesses make between $2 million to $20 million in revenue, Jim offers a peek into his day-to-day juggling tasks, ranging from marketing a business to negotiating deals to coordinating with lawyers and accountants to ensure a smooth transition. You'll understand why having a broker who wears many hats (Jim is known for his hat styling, by the way) is crucial in the business selling process.

■ **Jim, you are a business broker in Kingston, Ontario, Canada. Tell us about your work and the people you help.**

Jim Nairn: There are 30 different roles that I perform for my clients, between being a business broker and a business owner. In short, I help business owners understand the value that the market sees in their business today and whether or not now is a good time for them to take their business to market or whether they should try to grow it for a couple of years to potentially meet their retirement goals or the objectives of their next steps. I also help them market the business, find prospective buyers, help with the negotiations, and work with the closing teams, such as the lawyers and the accountants on both sides, to make everything happen as smoothly as possible. I help many entrepreneurs in Canada with a business earning between $2 million to $20 million in revenue who find that they don't have the time and/or expertise to be able to do this on their own, but they understand the need for it and are willing to put in some of the work. Even though I'm doing a lot of the heavy lifting, the business owners still have work to do themselves - to give me the information needed to make the sale possible.

■ **What is the biggest challenge your clients face?**

Jim Nairn: Quite often, time and stress are their biggest challenges. By bringing me on board, once we get the initial information that is needed to do my job, they can return to working on their business. I will take the time to develop all the marketing materials, vet the prospective buyers, etc., on their behalf. Then, I can bring them back to the table once we have some buyers in place who are a good fit for them and meet the prerequisites we've established. They can choose which ones they would like to meet. A lot of my job is freeing the owner from the actual work of the sale process, which would otherwise be a heavy burden for them.

◼ Are there common myths or misconceptions about selling a business?

Jim Nairn: Many business owners don't understand the amount of time or work involved, or they might think their accountant or lawyer can handle the sale for them. Unfortunately, those particular professionals, while they are needed for selling your business, aren't necessarily the best ones to help you market it and get the best selection of buyers for you because that isn't what they are trained to do. I solely focus on helping people buy and sell businesses. I don't focus on accounting or drafting legal documents because those things aren't in my job description.

Going back to the time component, many sellers don't understand how long it takes to develop marketing collateral properly, put all the information together, prepare for due diligence, and negotiate. Depending on the nature and size of the business, this can take anywhere from six to 24 months.

■ Are there any big mistakes or pitfalls you help business owners avoid when selling?

Jim Nairn: When business owners try to sell on their own, they don't understand what information the other side needs and why and when they need to provide it. Sometimes, they aren't concerned with confidentiality and shout from the rooftops, "Hey, I'm looking to sell my business. Do you know anybody that might want to buy it?" But meanwhile, that can have a very negative effect on the value of their business. We do our best to maintain confidentiality, which in turn maintains the value of the business.

Also, I often hear about scenarios where business owners will go out to lunch or participate in golf tournaments with other business owners. And they might run into the same person who always says, "Hey, when you are ready to sell your business, just let me know. I'll write you a check." But I've found 95% or more of these people are just blowing smoke. They don't have any real intentions of actually buying the business. Or at least every time I contact them, they say, "Oh, I'm not ready right now. If you had talked to me a couple of months ago before (insert excuse here) happened, I would have bought it with no problem!" That's not always the case, but it's what I'm hearing most often. So, I typically ask the business owners for a list of those types of people, and I'll contact them first to determine just how serious they are. But we will go to the regular market if they don't respond within a reasonable timeframe.

■ What inspired you to get started in this field?

Jim Nairn: I started when I was finishing my Masters at the Royal Military College of Canada here in Kingston. A friend of mine was working as a receptionist in the Sunbelt office, and she knew that I would need a career after the program was over, so she suggested I come and meet with the owner. After a few meetings and a little research, I joined the team about a year later as I was finishing my studies. Shortly after that, I bought into the office, and it was a totally new world for me regarding opportunity. I'm a big proponent of helping people where help doesn't exist. This was a perfect fit for me in that regard. I love witnessing the joy and relief of owners who successfully sell their businesses. There is often a physically noticeable change in their demeanor and personality once the dust settles from the sale of their business and their stress lifts; these signs tell me that the time was right for us to meet and for me to help them through the process. This is what keeps me going.

■ Is there anything else you would like to share with business owners?

Jim Nairn: If you are considering selling or buying a business, please look for a professional nearby with whom you can have a good relationship. There are more than just a handful of us in Canada now. The industry is growing. It's not quite what it is in the United States, but it's growing. So take the time to meet with a couple of different people and find the right fit for you. You would be hard-pressed not to find at least one person you could work well with. As long as you're getting professional help, that's all I can ask.

■ **How can people find you, connect with you, and learn more?**

Jim Nairn: It's easy enough to find me on LinkedIn. I'm also on the International Business Brokers Association of Canada and a few other associations. Just look me up on Google. You'll find the guy with the hat and the beard, which will likely be me!

JIM NAIRN, MBA, MCBI

〜━━━━━━━〜

Master Certified Business Intermediary

**Sunbelt Business Brokers Bizcap
Brokerage, Sunbelt Kingston**

Even though Jim became aware of the business brokerage world through a friend many years ago while completing his Master's, he has taken to it with great enthusiasm. The idea of helping entrepreneurs through the complex and often emotional process of buying and selling their businesses and witnessing their relief and jubilation upon a successful transition is a driving force for Jim.

It is an unfortunate reality that issues will arise during the process of purchasing or selling a business. Sometimes, these can take a toll on people's emotions and cause extra stress. During those stressful times, Jim encourages his clients to vent about the process and what's going on, after which he empathetically verifies what is happening and the alternatives/options and offers suggestions on how to best proceed based upon his client's goals.

Being an advocate for lifelong learning is a bonus for Jim as the business brokerage world allows him to continuously build upon his education and experience so that he can better service his client's needs. He routinely signs up for additional learning opportunities beyond the numerous courses required to maintain his memberships and designations related to the various industry organizations he belongs to.

Please do not hesitate to contact Jim for your buying or selling needs.

Industry Associations

Member of the International Business Brokers Association
Member of the International Business Brokers Association of Canada
Member of the Mergers & Acquisitions Source
Member of the International Society of Business Appraisers
Member of the Real Estate Council of Ontario

Education

Royal Military College of Canada – MBA, Business (2014)

Laurentian University – BBA, Business Administration (2011)

St. Lawrence College – Business Administration, Marketing Diploma (2000)

EMAIL:

jim.nairn@sunbeltcanada.com

PHONE:

(613) 549-7774

WEBSITE:

https://www.sunbeltcanada.com/kingston/

JIM M. PEAKE

REHAB REVEALED: PREPARING YOUR FACILITY FOR A SUCCESSFUL SALE

Conversation with Jim M. Peake

In this interview, we speak with Jim M. Peake, the founder of Addiction-Rep.com, a leading advisory service in the behavioral health field. Jim has dedicated his expertise to assisting addiction treatment centers, senior living facilities, and drug testing labs in navigating the complexities of healthcare mergers and acquisitions. He shares his clients' unique challenges, debunks common myths, and offers advice for those looking to sell their healthcare facilities. Whether you're a seasoned professional or new to the industry, Jim's insights provide a comprehensive understanding of this niche market.

■ **Tell us about your work and the people you help.**

Jim M. Peake: I am the founder of Addiction-Rep. We are seasoned veterans in our specific fields and skill sets who have combined professional services and advisory services for the behavioral health field, which includes addiction treatment, senior living facilities, and drug testing labs. And they're all interrelated. Addiction treatment centers and senior living centers house patients, and they either send out to drug testing labs or are large enough to house the drug testing labs inside the facility.

■ **What are the biggest challenges your clients face? How do you help them overcome these challenges?**

Jim M. Peake: The healthcare field has many challenges. In the mergers and acquisitions space, we help these companies with funding. For example, they might need to add another 20 beds to the facility or buy a new location.

Finding buyers for a business is important. Typically, sellers do not want to put their business on a public business broker directory website. They'd rather do it discreetly by hiring a professional like myself or one of my other competitors in the space. They prefer a more rifle-shot approach, where we call specific people in our niche market interested in expanding to a new market. These usually end up being referrals who convert and convert well. We refer to these as strategic acquisitions for the purchasing company. They may want another intensive outpatient facility in a specific area or another senior living facility in a different state. So, we use our network to reach those folks.

The other problem all these facilities are having is staffing. We know that people are overworked. Many regulatory things are happening in the space, which equals filling out more paperwork. It puts a lot of added stress everywhere in the healthcare space.

■ Are there any myths or misconceptions about selling these types of facilities?

Jim M. Peake: I like to say that somebody must have issued a memo to people who are brand new coming into the space that drug rehab facilities are "get rich quick" businesses. Many people jumped into the senior living space two dozen years ago as they saw that expanding as the hot market, and the rehab space soon followed. They all thought it was easy to buy a rehab facility and you would get rich fast. That's not the case. There are so many moving parts. You have to be concerned about the billing, whether you're doing it in-house or hiring it out and being paid by insurance. But first, you want to be in the insurance game, especially in drug rehab. Several senior living spaces have insurance, but it's not big monthly money like in the drug rehab space.

Then you have to focus on things like marketing; how do you fill these beds, whether it be in a senior living facility or whether it be in a drug rehab? The turnover of a rehab detox bed is anywhere from three to four days. You must fill a space in a residential treatment center every 14, 28, or 45 days. The patients only stick around briefly since they step down to a different service, such as an Intensive Outpatient (IOP) or Partial Hospitalization Program (PHP). So, since there is high turnover, it costs money to keep filling the funnel. And it costs money, whether you pay warm human beings to knock on doors of interventionists, hospitals, lawyer's offices, and police stations to get people in or whether you're paying a digital marketing firm to generate phone calls through Google My Business, search engine optimization (SEO), or (PPC) pay per click advertising like Google Adwords. Those are all expensive ways to generate leads, and you have to hire professionals to do it, either in-house or out-of-house. You must also keep up with regulatory issues and certifications such as JCAHO accreditation and CARF accreditation.

None of this stuff is complicated, but there are just a lot of moving parts at the same time. So that's the challenge. And if you don't have experience in the space, it's almost like playing a game of Whack-a-Mole; you might put out one fire on the insurance side, but then you have another problem on the marketing side, or you have another issue on the clinical side. You might have somebody leave against medical advice (AMA), meaning they check in and then walk out the front door two days later. That's a real problem; all kinds of reports must be filled out when something like this happens.

The other myth is sellers think it will only take 30 to 60 days to sell their business because they have all their ducks in a row, have their financials prepared, and have all their licenses and leases ready. But a sale can get very complicated. Typically, many of these projects take anywhere from four to six months. I've even had sales take 15 months, which is a long time. The due diligence process with billing and insurance is extensive, and you will be going through an auditing type of process, whether you like it or not, during the due diligence phase.

■ What are common mistakes or pitfalls you help your clients avoid when selling their facility?

Jim M. Peake: One of the first things would be commingling their personal and business funds. That's a big one. Many are lifestyle businesses where their whole family is on the insurance program, or the owner might have bought another car for their spouse or child. So it's important to keep track of that stuff and prepare the financials to add those things back.

Consistent and steady admissions are also a challenge because of all the market factors, including seasonality. Rehabs do not have many admissions around the Christmas holidays, but there tends to be an uptick after the new year. Lead generation is a critical activity for all rehabs and senior living centers.

Staffing consistency has always been challenging since clinicians can walk out the door, and replacing them is not always easy. The staff is typically overworked and finds themselves filling out a lot of paperwork. Also, they get burned out and sometimes run out of empathy. If your rehab or senior living facility is in far-away Montana, it doesn't have the same labor pool as Malibu or West Palm Beach.

Building trust is a game changer. It starts with branding. Branding is something that many people sleep on because a lot of these rehabs sound the same, like Drug Rehab in North Carolina and Drug Rehab in Texas. After a while, you glaze over because they don't have well-known names like Betty Ford, Caron, or Sierra Tucson. There aren't many centers that have done a great job with branding. I started in the professional marketing space, so I know firsthand how much goodwill branding adds to a business's value. Reputation creates trust. Trust will convert a website visitor to a phone call, and trust formed from the phone call talking to the admissions director will get the person to come in and become an admit. It's all about trust.

■ What inspired you to get into this line of work?

Jim M. Peake: Long story short, I have been involved with the Internet since 1995, so almost 30 years. Fast forward to 2008, I was working with a healthcare magazine publishing company, and they asked me to build an ad network for them. So, I did that, and when the project expired, I was looking for my next gig. One of the advertisers in that ad network happened to be a drug rehab directory. He asked me if I could help him build his business. And I thought, "You know what, that sounds like a great opportunity." It sounded like a great opportunity to me because I was talking to another mentor of mine named Glenn Livingston, who is a professional marketing guy. He recommended that if you're going to be in the marketing game, you need to niche it down into something very specific. And I figured drug rehab healthcare is a niche, so let me take it on! Glenn went to the outer reaches of delivering on niche marketing by getting into the alpaca blanket market to prove a point about the importance of choosing a niche. And so I saw that niche opportunity and went for it. That's how I ended up in the drug rehab space.

■ Is there anything else you would like to share with potential sellers?

Jim M. Peake: Valuation, valuation, valuation. You must understand where the market is. And we do that by doing research. Some people who don't understand the business side might overvalue what their business is worth. In other cases, they don't think the business is worth that much, but it's worth a ton of money. So, getting a third party to do a valuation is highly recommended. That's something we provide as a professional service for fair market value.

To accompany it, I would tell everyone to get their books audited by a CPA. You must be able to track the money because whoever buys your treatment center will audit your books. If you do it ahead of time, you'll close the deal much faster and probably get a higher valuation if you have your ducks in a row.

I also advise getting and paying for competent legal counsel. Lawyers should make you money. Governance is another topic that comes up before, during, and after the sale of a business. Real estate is a huge part of the rehab and senior living businesses. Sometimes, the real estate might be in a different LLC with different owners than the actual business itself. Ensuring all the partners are on board with the transaction makes sense. If not, you will have a problem.

If you are a rehab business and you are taking in or subscribing a lot of friends and family you must make sure that your cap table is dialed in and who owns what, what percentage, what class shares they have etc. Ideally, you do this long before you sell the business.

Billing is a place where rehabs can save literally millions of dollars. As the technology improves, many of the EMRs offer billing types of services. If you are going to do this, you want your internal team to be able to manage the billing correctly. It takes experience, knowledge, and training. We provide those services where you can bring your billing in-house, and we will get you up to speed quickly, and you won't have to deal with a ton of reimbursement denials.

Lastly, I recommend that you use a combination of digital online marketing and on-the-ground marketing. You must keep your pipeline full. A rehab business that has a full pipeline will have consistent revenue and income. Both income sources cost money. If you aren't where you want to be financially today, invest in both or at least one.

If you expect your business to be successful with a 1.5% marketing budget to the top-line revenue proforma, you will be in for a world of hurt, especially if you are just beginning. The pros have their marketing dialed in and have the reports, and the admits to prove it. Make sure you have this humming before you sell.

■ **How can people find you, connect with you, and learn more?**

Jim M. Peake: You can Google my name or visit my websites at healthcare-rep.com or addiction-rep.com.

• Invite people into the conversation
  with you and learn more.

JIM M. PEAKE

Founder, Business Broker

Healthcare-Rep Inc.

Jim Peake started in the direct mail industry in 1982. Fast forward to 1995, he saw the direct response power of the Internet and joined a super fast-growing dot.com in Silicon Alley in NYC. One of his notable accomplishments was the design and delivery of IBM's international chess event in 1996: Kasparov vs. IBM's Deep Blue supercomputer. Garry Kasparov beat the supercomputer. Fast forward to 2008, Jim entered the addiction treatment field by joining an addiction treatment directory.

From there, he began a consulting company that helped drug rehabs with their digital marketing and website development. Many call this type of marketing "putting heads in beds." Along the way, Jim began buying and selling behavioral health companies, commonly known as drug rehabs.

Jim saw many opportunities in the addiction treatment field specifically to help the rehabs offer stronger solutions, lower costs as well as increased income and revenue, so he embarked on Healthcare-Rep Inc. Healthcare-Rep Inc. offers the following services:

1. M&A Services & Advisory
   a. Providing valuations
   b. M&A services
   c. Selling drug rehabs
2. Real Estate Services
   a. Zoning & Licensing
   b. Real Estate Buying & Selling
   c. Property Detail Reports, Broker Price Opinions, Appraisals
   d. Location Analytics & Demographic Profiles
3. Management Services
   a. Strategic Planning and Consulting
   b. Rehab & Senior Living Consulting
   c. Leadership Program
   d. Operations Execution - Company Turnarounds

4. Technical Services

    a. Bring Billing in House

    b. Compliance

    c. Collections for out-of-network insurance and RCM

    d. Custom Software Development

5. Revenue Generating Services

    a. World Class Branding

    b. Website Development & Maintenance

    c. SEO/SEM Marketing/Branding

    d. Call Tracking

    e. Article writing and content creation for websites

EMAIL:

jim@jimpeake.com

PHONE:

781-222-0000 Cell

WEBSITES:

https://healthcare-rep.com/
https://addiction-rep.com/

YATIN THAKORE

FROM LABS TO RICHES

Conversation with Yatin Thakore

Yatin Thakore transforms challenges into opportunities for entrepreneurs transitioning out of their businesses. With an initial background as a research scientist, Yatin's career turned towards mergers and acquisitions when he was approached to sell a laboratory. Recognizing a niche in aiding small to medium-sized labs and related sectors in navigating the sale process, Yatin and his partners founded TechnologyPark.com. They carved out a unique space in the market, specializing in businesses typically ranging from one to twenty million dollars in revenue. In this interview, Yatin discusses the nuances of business valuation, the importance of preparation, and the common misconceptions surrounding the sale of a business. His insights are invaluable for any business owner contemplating the sale of their most significant asset.

■ **Yatin, you are a managing partner and certified value builder advisor at TechnologyPark.com. Tell us about your work and the people you help.**

Yatin Thakore: I was a research scientist who worked in research laboratories for many years. Around 2010, my two partners and I started consulting, helping small laboratories with interesting products and technologies. We would help them license their products or get funding for them.

Then, one day, a lab owner came to us and asked if we would help him sell his lab since we knew everything that goes on in one. So, we accidentally got into the M&A space. And we realized that we were quite good at it. It was a time when few people were helping small- to medium-sized laboratories with the sales process or finding buyers. Many of these owners were scientists, so they didn't know much about the sale process or how to go about it. Investment banks usually worked on much larger deals and retainers. We realized that there was a gap in the marketplace, and so we chose this niche area. Soon afterward, we set up a marketplace called LaboratoryForSale. com. And since we were so niche, we were always on the first page of Google, which resulted in more and more business.

We started helping small- and medium-sized lab owners sell their laboratories. Slowly, we expanded into related areas like medical businesses, healthcare businesses, and the IT space. Our sweet spot is typically between one to 20 million dollars in revenue. But we also have helped smaller businesses. It has been a lot of fun helping entrepreneurs exit their businesses. Often, they don't even realize they are sitting on the most valuable asset they have.

■ What is the biggest challenge your clients face? How do you help them overcome this challenge?

Yatin Thakore: Most business owners have never sold a business. You probably don't know how to sell a business unless you are a serial entrepreneur. Business owners also typically don't know what their businesses are worth. And they may not realize it, but a business can be worth a lot more than a home! Sometimes, the business may not be quite ready for selling, so we provide education on how to make the business more sellable and valuable.

■ Are there common myths and misconceptions about selling a business?

Yatin Thakore: We hear things like, "Hey, my buddy sold his business for 7x multiple, so I should be able to get that!" However, all businesses are different, and one size does not fit all. Also, people must realize how much time and preparation it takes to sell a business. You can't just throw a bunch of financials together and say, "Find me a buyer." It's much deeper than that.

■ **Can you shed some light on the different variables people need to consider when it comes to valuation?**

Yatin Thakore: Multiples are a widely used matrix. Depending on the type of business, there are often multiples of cash flow, or more precisely, in the M&A jargon, EBITDA (earnings before interest, taxes, depreciation, and amortization). For smaller businesses, they could be multiples of the seller's discretionary earnings. But a lot goes into determining the multiple. If the business is larger, they can typically get larger multiples. It also depends on factors like the quality of the management team, the business's growth potential, and how dependent the business is on one particular customer or vendor. Larger businesses get higher multiples because they typically have a management team, better accounting system, etc. As a Value Builder advisor, I often teach business owners about the eight factors determining the business's value and scalability. We offer a free Value Builder Score that they can get by answering a few questions to see how well they're doing in each of those eight areas.

■ **What common mistakes or pitfalls do you help people avoid when selling their businesses?**

Yatin Thakore: It's very important to gather the required information upfront before putting the business on the market. In an ideal scenario, the business owner should prepare for the sale at least one or two years or more in advance. During this time, the accountant should review and prepare the financials. Many small businesses count personal expenses, such as vacations or household expenses, as business expenses. They do this to reduce taxes. But this hurts the business's profits, so they show much lower profits when ready to sell. Usually, when we prepare financial statements, we can "add back" certain types of personal expenses. But if the owner has been adding a lot of other expenses into business expenses, it will not be possible to count many of these into "add-backs." For example, let's say that they added $100,000 of personal expenses as business expenses, showing that their business profit is $100,000 less than it is. At the 30% tax bracket, they would save $30,000 in taxes (unless, of course, the IRS catches them). Now, they are selling their business, and the valuation is four times the cash flow (EBITDA). So, $100,000 less profit in the business means they get $400,000 less when they sell! Against $30,000 saved in taxes! As the saying goes - this is being "penny-wise and pound-foolish!"

So the best thing is to keep the financials clean. Don't mix personal expenses with business expenses. You will get better value, and you will also sleep better.

Also, once you put your business up for sale, be prepared to spend a lot of time moving the process along. If buyers ask questions, don't wait weeks before providing answers because they will lose interest.

■ Is there anything else you want to share with business owners considering selling?

Yatin Thakore: Remember that unless you pass your business down to a family member, you *will* be selling at some point. It's essential to keep the end in mind and make your business desirable for buyers so it is sellable and valuable as an asset. Just like you look after your other investments, such as stocks, you should pay attention to making your business the most valuable it can be. As a certified value builder advisor, I know how to make your business more desirable and valuable. We have a free value builder score questionnaire, and in 20 minutes, you can get a benchmark number, which gives you an idea of where you are in the eight categories of factors that increase value. We also offer a free 30-minute consultation to explain the score, the areas that need more work, and what you can do to improve to ensure a much higher value for your business and more buyers who will be interested.

■ How can people find you, connect with you, and learn more?

Yatin Thakore: You can find me on LinkedIn at https://www.linkedin.com/in/ythakore/ or email me at ythakore@technologypark.com.

YATIN B. THAKORE, PH.D., CBI, CM&AA

Managing Partner, Certified Value Builder Advisor

TechnologyPark.com

Yatin has multidisciplinary experience in the chemical, medical/ healthcare, and IT industries. He has spent many years in senior roles as a research scientist and has several patents in the diagnostic areas, which were licensed to a major pharma company. Yatin has worked in Fortune 100 companies (Bendix Corp, now Allied Corporation), JP Morgan Chase, and very early start-ups. He also started a dot.com company in the early days of the Internet.

He has been active in the Merger and Acquisition area for the past ten years. He is the founder/partner of TechnologyPark.com, a niche M&A Advisory firm that focuses on Laboratory, Medical, and IT businesses. As a scientist, Yatin understood the laboratory and medical space and saw a need to help small- and medium-sized laboratory owners find lucrative exits. As a result, his company has created LaboratoryForSale.com, a highly visible marketplace for selling laboratories and businesses that sell products and services in the laboratory and healthcare space. Since then, the company has also created several other marketplaces for the Imaging Centers (ImagingCenters4Sale.com) and other Medical and IT businesses. As a Certified Value Builder Advisor, Yatin coaches companies to become more valuable and sellable.

Yatin holds a Ph.D. and Master's in Materials Science and Engineering from the University of Utah and a B.Tech in Chemical Engineering from the Indian Institute of Technology, Mumbai. In his spare time, Yatin loves to travel, go for hikes, read (particularly business books), listen to podcasts, see movies and plays (once in a while, binge-watching on cable channels), and spend time with family and friends.

EMAIL:

ythakore@technologypark.com

WEBSITE:

https://TechnologyPark.com

PHONE:

+1-732-390-7435

LINKEDIN:

https://www.linkedin.com/in/ythakore/

CLAUDIO VILAS

RAISING THE ROOF ON BUSINESS SALES

Conversation with Claudio Vilas

Claudio Vilas stands out as a specialized expert dedicated to assisting roofing business owners in selling their businesses. With a deep understanding of the roofing industry's intricacies, Claudio has built a reputation for his strategic approach and commitment to securing the best outcomes for his clients. In this interview, Claudio shares his insights on the key factors that attract buyers to roofing businesses, the common challenges owners face during the sale process, and the strategies that have led to successful transactions under his guidance.

■ Tell us about your work and the people you help.

Claudio Vilas: My work is selling businesses, specifically roofing companies. I haven't sold anything else since last year. The clients I help are business owners in their 50s or 60s looking to retire and wanting to exit their companies. On the other hand, young business owners want to grow their businesses and need investment. Either one is a good client for me, and I love helping them because they bring jobs to society. So whether you're retiring or a younger person needing investment in your company, I can help.

> ■ **What is the biggest challenge that these business owners face when it comes to selling their business? How do you help them overcome this challenge?**

Claudio Vilas: The biggest challenge is that when you're running a business, you're not asking the same questions a buyer would ask. There's a big discrepancy between what a professional buyer looks for and what the business owner is prepared to provide. I don't like to sell businesses to people who are not ready to buy them. Professional buyers are looking for information that business owners are not necessarily prepared to provide, and I help them get ready for that situation.

Typically, there are issues with how they have their accounting set up or how they keep track of the different KPIs of their companies. Business owners look at their business from the exact opposite side a buyer does. When you talk with a business owner, they'll tell you about their sales or marketing strategies, but when you ask, "How much money are you making?" you often get a deer-in-the-head-lights look. They might not have an exact answer, but this is the first question a buyer will ask. Once you answer that, the buyer wants to know how you make that money, diving into marketing, sales, production, etc. It sometimes takes me a few months to get to that answer.

Many owners believe they can sell their business quickly because they get emails from people claiming they want to buy it. They think they can get it ready at the snap of a finger. But that's not the case. I help them prepare the business for sale and ensure we have the right information for the buyers.

■ **What are some of the biggest myths or misconceptions about selling a business, particularly roofing companies?**

Claudio Vilas: There are a couple of important myths. First is the multiples. I get people calling me saying their neighbor sold his company for ten times EBITDA, but that's only the case if you're in technology or venture capital, where you're starting a new company that will change the world. Typically, you'll sell your business based on how much money it's making. The multiple can vary between one and two to five or six or seven or eight, but when you get to those higher multiples, you're looking at businesses making ten million dollars or more in EBITDA. People often have unrealistic expectations because they heard someone sold their business for a high multiple.

Another misconception is that the best deal comes from someone who emails you out of the blue. Many of those emails are spam sent to hundreds or thousands of business owners. To sell your business properly, you need a strategy that includes bringing several buyers to bid for it, not just accepting the first offer you get.

Business owners also often think they must leave their businesses once they sell them. No, you can sell the business and stay, sometimes making more money by doing so!

Finally, some believe they can sell the business themselves, but you need a team of professionals, including attorneys, accountants, wealth managers, and tax people. Watching a YouTube video won't replace professional expertise.

■ What are the biggest mistakes or pitfalls that you see roofing companies make when trying to sell their businesses?

Claudio Vilas: The number one mistake is believing that an unsolicited email offer is the best they can get.

Another mistake is relying too much on their own knowledge to sell the business, forgetting they need professionals to help them. Trying to save money by not paying a broker can cost them a lot more. They often lose out on potential higher offers and better terms because they don't have professional support.

Confidentiality is also crucial. You risk exposing your business's information if you go directly to buyers without the right NDAs and protections.

■ What inspired you to get into this line of work?

Claudio Vilas: I'm a huge advocate for entrepreneurship and small businesses. Small businesses drive 80% of our economy. I believe that helping small business owners is the best way to give back to society. Many small business owners are at a disadvantage because they don't have the right advice or support. YouTube and online "gurus" have made it easy for anyone to give advice, but this often lacks depth and professionalism.

Business owners put everything on the line, including their personal and family investments. They can lose everything quickly due to unexpected events like a pandemic. I want to help them maximize their return on investment and keep their legacy intact. My goal is not only to focus on the transaction itself but also to keep as much money as possible from the sale by working on tax strategies and deal structures. You don't have to ride into the sunset after selling your company; you can stay involved and benefit from it in the future if you do the right deal and work with professionals.

■ **Is there anything else you want to share with roofing company owners considering selling?**

Claudio Vilas: The roofing industry is in a seller's market today. Big companies are looking to buy roofing businesses; owners can sell for a good multiple. Even if it's not ten times EBITDA, it's still an excellent time to sell. If you don't prepare your company for sale now, you might face stiffer competition in the future from businesses sold to larger companies. These larger companies will have better access to resources and professionals. Even if you're not ready to sell today, it's a good time to start preparing your company for sale.

■ **How can people find you, connect with you, and learn more?**

Claudio Vilas: They can call my cell phone at 954-774-4141 or email me at claudio.vilas@sunbeltnetwork.com. My website is www.theroofingbizbroker.com.

CLAUDIO VILAS

Roofing Business Broker and M&A Advisor

Sunbelt Business Brokers of South Florida

With a specialized focus on selling construction businesses, Claudio Vilas stands out as a premier business broker dedicated to transforming business owners' legacies into significant financial rewards. Based in Florida and serving clients nationwide, Claudio brings a wealth of experience and a robust network to ensure successful transactions for his clients.

Claudio's expertise lies in meticulously preparing businesses for sale, leveraging deep sector knowledge, particularly in the roofing industry. He understands this niche's unique challenges and opportunities, making him the go-to advisor for roofing business owners looking to maximize their earnings. His comprehensive approach includes thorough business analysis, strategic deal structuring, and connecting with qualified buyers, primarily Private Equity Groups (PEGs) eager to invest in the sector.

Committed to confidentiality and professionalism, Claudio ensures that sensitive information is protected throughout the sale process. His services are tailored to meet the specific needs of his clients, from enhancing business value to navigating complex market dynamics. Claudio's innovative methods and use of the latest technology make the process smooth, efficient, and effective.

Beyond his professional achievements, Claudio is passionate about entrepreneurship, business, libertarianism, personal development, and capitalism. He enjoys traveling and sailing, and he finds inspiration in experiencing new places and cultures.

Claudio Vilas' tagline, "Your Legacy, My Commitment," reflects his dedication to preserving and enhancing the hard-earned legacies of business owners, securing their future while ensuring they achieve the highest possible value for their businesses.

EMAIL:
Claudio.vilas@sunbeltnetwork.com

PHONE:
(954) 774-4141

WEBSITE:
www.theroofingbizbroker.com

FACEBOOK:
https://www.facebook.com/ClaudiovilasBB

ABOUT THE PUBLISHER

MARK IMPERIAL is a best-selling author who learned the art of influential writing through his work with Dan S. Kennedy. He was one of the chosen few that Dan personally certified as an Independent Business Advisor in 2008. Mark has gone on to help over 600 professionals publish their client-attracting books in fields like Financial Planning, Family Law, Elder Law, and Business Exit Planning, to name a few.

Mark discovered the power of books that sell things when he wrote a pet iguana care book that sold over 50 iguanas every Sunday at a flea market, yielding $1,500+ before noon. He repeated that success by writing a wedding entertainment book that attracted clients to his DJ service and booked it solid year after year. This inspired Mark to share his love of crafting authority-defining books with business owners and professionals worldwide.

Currently residing in the western suburbs of Chicago, Mark shares his home with the love of his life Shannon, bonus children Max and Felix (who he affectionately refers to as "the chuckleheads"), a turtle, a bearded dragon, and Fortune, his beloved French Bulldog. When Mark isn't being a marketing nerd, he practices martial arts, keeps up with Shannon on her bicycle, eats Thai food, and watches his favorite TV show - infomercials. Visit: www.BooksGrowBusiness. com for more.

www.ingramcontent.com/pod-product-compliance
Lightning Source LLC
Chambersburg PA
CBHW070933210326
41520CB00021B/6929